The
SMALL and MIGHTY
Book of
Bears

Published in 2023 by OH!,
An imprint of Welbeck Children's Limited, part of Welbeck Publishing Group
Offices in: London – 20 Mortimer Street, London W1T 3JW
and Sydney – 205 Commonwealth Street, Surry Hills 2010
www.welbeckpublishing.com

Design and layout © Welbeck Children's Limited 2023
Text copyright © Welbeck Children's Limited 2023

All rights reserved. No part of this publication may be reproduced, stored in
a retrieval system, or transmitted in any form or by any means, electronically,
mechanical, photocopying, recording, or otherwise, without the prior
permission of the copyright owners and the publishers.

A CIP record for this book is available from the Library of Congress.

Writer: Catherine Brereton
Illustrator: Isabel Muñoz
Consultant: Paul Lawston
Design and editorial by Raspberry Books Ltd
Editorial Manager: Tash Mosheim
Design Manager: Russell Porter
Production: Jess Brisley

ISBN 978 1 80069 465 1

Printed in Heshan, China

10 9 8 7 6 5 4 3 2 1

FSC
www.fsc.org
MIX
Paper | Supporting
responsible forestry
FSC® C020056

The
SMALL and MIGHTY
Book of
Bears

Catherine Brereton and Isabel Muñoz

Contents

INTRODUCTION

This little book is absolutely bulging with facts about bears.

Bears are large, intelligent animals. They are fierce hunters, but they're also friendly-looking, so we find them both frightening and adorable at the same time.

All bears have a large body with stocky legs, shaggy fur coats, and a short, bushy tail. They have small, round ears, no whiskers, and big paws, each with five claws.

Step into this book and you will meet . . .

🐾 a bear with a mouth like
a vacuum cleaner

🐾 an acrobatic bear that does handstands

🐾 bears that make faces at each other

🐾 a bear that became a soldier

. . . and lots more.

Read on for an adventure with some of
the world's most roar-some creatures.

Types
of
Bear

THERE ARE **EIGHT** DIFFERENT TYPES, OR SPECIES, OF BEAR IN THE WORLD.

Polar bear

NORTH AMERICA

Brown bear

North American black bear

North American black bear

THE **SPECTACLED BEAR** lives the **FARTHEST SOUTH** in world.

Spectacled bear

SOUTH AMERICA

Brown bear

Brown bear

Brown bear

Brown bear

Giant panda

EUROPE

ASIA

Asiatic
black bear

AFRICA

Sloth bear

Sun bear

There are
NO BEARS at all
in AFRICA
or AUSTRALIA.

AUSTRALIA

11

THE DIFFERENT BEARS LINE UP BIGGEST TO SMALLEST LIKE THIS:

(These sizes are the shoulder height of a male bear.)

Polar bear
5 ft. 3 in

Brown bear
4 ft. 11 in

North American black bear 3 ft. 5 in

Sloth bear 3 ft

Asiatic black bear 3 ft. 3 in

Giant panda 2 ft. 4 in

Spectacled bear 3 ft

Sun bear 2 ft. 4 in

～ THE ～
POLAR BEAR
is the biggest bear. It's the
largest land carnivore on Earth.

Polar bears live in the **Arctic**, one of the world's coldest environments. They roam across ice and swim through icy seas.

More than **TWO-THIRDS** of the world's polar bears live in **CANADA**.

THERE ARE MANY DIFFERENT VARIETIES OF BROWN BEAR. THEY INCLUDE:

Gobi bear

Himalayan brown bear

Amur brown bear

Kamchatka bear

and Eurasian brown bear

∽

IN NORTH AMERICA THERE ARE:

Alaskan brown bear

Kodiak bear

North American brown bear

(or grizzly bear)

GRIZZLY BEARS

get their name because their brown fur is silver-tipped or "grizzled."

Brown bears roam across vast areas of forests, woodlands, mountainside meadows, and prairies.

Today, because the **global climate** is **changing**, polar bears and North American brown bears are **wandering** into **each other's** territory more often.

Sometimes they **BREED** with each other. Their cubs are known as "**GROLAR**" or "**PIZZLY**" bears.

NORTH AMERICAN
BLACK BEARS ARE
NOT ALWAYS BLACK.
THEY CAN BE:

Black

Blond

Brown

Blue-grey

Reddish-brown

White

In the west of the USA, where there are **open meadows** and the **weather** is hot, you find more **light-colored bears**.

In the northeast, where there is more **forest** and it is **colder**, they are nearly all **black**.

SUN BEARS

are found in Southeast Asia.
They have short fur,
which helps them keep cool in
the tropical
rainforests
where they
live.

They get their name
because they sometimes
have a pattern on their chest
that looks a bit like a SUN.

SUN BEARS
LOVE
TO EAT HONEY,
SO ARE ALSO
CALLED **HONEY**
BEARS.

SLOTH BEARS

have LONG, THICK CLAWS like a sloth and sometimes hang upside down on tree branches like sloths do. But they are agile and can run fast.

There is a Y-shaped mark on a sloth bear's chest.

SLOTH BEARS ARE THE **ONLY** BEARS THAT ARE MORE **ACTIVE** AT **NIGHT.**

GIANT PANDAS are

unusual among
bears because
they don't eat meat.
Well, hardly.
Almost all their diet
is made up of

BAMBOO,

but the occasional
insect creeps in.

Scientists think that many millions of years ago the panda would have eaten meat. Like other bears it has **the POWERFUL JAWS of** a meat-eater.

᠊ᢍ᠊

Pandas POOP about 40 TIMES A DAY.

THE SPECTACLED BEAR

gets its name from the markings on its face, which make it look like it is wearing spectacles.

28

It lives in the
ANDES MOUNTAINS
of South America
and spends most of its
time up in the TREES.

Spectacled bears have been seen
sitting in trees for several days
waiting for fruit to ripen.

Although it is one of the smaller
bears, and although it is mainly
vegetarian, the spectacled bear is
South America's biggest meat-eater.

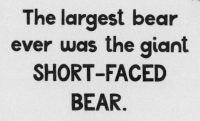

The largest bear
ever was the giant
**SHORT-FACED
BEAR.**

It lived throughout
North America from
1.6 million to 11,000 years
ago. It stood up to 6 feet
at shoulder height.

Scientists have worked out that the giant short-faced bear could RUN over 40 mph, FASTER than any MODERN BEAR.

31

Bears' Bodies

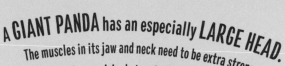

A **GIANT PANDA** has an especially **LARGE HEAD.**
The muscles in its jaw and neck need to be extra strong—
bamboo is surprisingly tough to gnaw and chew!

Bears have
BIG BRAINS for
their body size.

A GRIZZLY BEAR bites down with enough force to CRUSH a BOWLING BALL.

⌐ A ⌐

GRIZZLY BEAR
has a very round face.

If you look at it from the
side, you can see a curved
bowl shape.

36

A

BLACK BEAR
has a pointed face,
more like a dog's.

From the side, its
snout looks straight.

Grizzlies
have small, round ears
whereas black bears have
bigger, pointy ears.

37

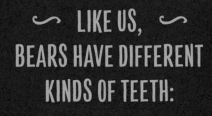

LIKE US, BEARS HAVE DIFFERENT KINDS OF TEETH:

- Some for snipping off plants and cutting meat—"incisors."

- Long sharp "canines" for slicing and ripping meat.

- Some, called "molars," for grinding plants.

They have a gap in between some of the teeth, which is useful for GRIPPING and SHREDDING LEAVES from a STEM.

Most adult bears have 42 teeth. Sloth bears have 40.

PANDAS ARE WELL KNOWN FOR THEIR "PANDA EYES"

—black patches around their eyes that give them their adorable look.

But the eyes themselves are different from those of other bears. Their pupils are vertical slits, like cats' eyes. Other bears have round pupils.

Scientists think that pandas' black-and-white face markings help other pandas recognize each other.

∽ THE ∽
SUN BEAR
has a REALLY LONG TONGUE—
up to 10 in long!

It uses
this long, strong
tongue to slurp up
honey from bees'
nests.

42

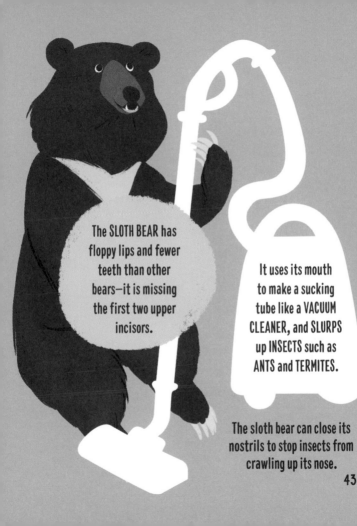

The SLOTH BEAR has floppy lips and fewer teeth than other bears—it is missing the first two upper incisors.

It uses its mouth to make a sucking tube like a VACUUM CLEANER, and SLURPS up INSECTS such as ANTS and TERMITES.

The sloth bear can close its nostrils to stop insects from crawling up its nose.

43

Brown bears have huge shoulder muscles, which make them very strong. The muscles are so big that they give the bear an obvious hump, which is one way of telling them apart from other bears.

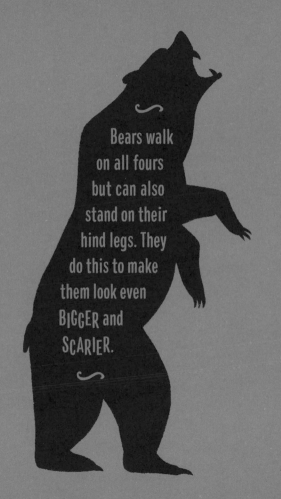

Bears walk
on all fours
but can also
stand on their
hind legs. They
do this to make
them look even
BIGGER and
SCARIER.

45

A bear's paw has five toes with sharp claws. Its front paws are bigger and stronger than its back paws.

A BEAR'S PAWS MATCH ITS LIFESTYLE:

SLOTH BEAR— long claws, used for digging.

BLACK BEAR— short, curved claws, good for climbing.

A grizzly bear's CLAWS can be as long as an adult human's finger!

GRIZZLY BEAR—
long, curved claws,
for digging up roots, insects,
and digging winter dens.

POLAR BEAR— partly
webbed, for swimming, with
black pads covered in tiny
bumps to stop them from
sliding around and claws to stop
them from slipping on the ice.

PANDA—
an extra "finger" on its
front paws, for holding
on to bamboo stems
while eating.

47

BEARS' FRONT PAWS MAKE FEARSOME WEAPONS.

A grizzly bear's long, sharp claws and its immense shoulder strength combine to make a slashing weapon that can kill prey as big as a moose in one swipe.

Bears have **pads** on the **underside** of their feet. These act like a cushion to protect the bears' feet from ground that is rough or too hot or too cold.

Sometimes,
black bears **LOSE THEIR
PADS** in **WINTER** when they are
HIBERNATING. Sometimes they
even eat the pads that
have come off!

A polar bear
has very large, round
paws—12 in wide.
The paws act like snowshoes for the
bear, spreading its weight so
it can walk on thin ice without
falling through it.

POLAR BEARS have **two layers** of **fur**— one of short, thick hair and another of longer, **waterproof** hair. Underneath the skin is a thick layer of fat, called BLUBBER. These do such a good job of keeping the bear warm that polar bears can get too hot when they run fast, even in icy temperatures.

50

The polar bear's fur
is not white!
Its hairs are actually see-through,
but appear white because light bounces
around the hollow hairs and this looks
white to our eyes. Underneath,
its skin is black.

The sun bear has the SHORTEST FUR so it can keep cool in the TROPICAL RAINFORESTS where it lives. The sloth bear, which lives in the MOUNTAINS, has the SHAGGIEST FUR.

Each hair of a grizzly bear's coat and found a total of 2,652 per square inch! This makes it extra warm. One scientist has counted the hairs on a grizzly bear's fur is VERY CURLY. This makes it extra warm. One scientist has counted the hairs on a grizzly bear's coat and found a total of 2,652 per square inch!

Hunting and Feeding

BEARS HAVE EXCELLENT SENSES

to help them find food. They have sharp eyesight, good hearing, and a great sense of smell.

Bears have a **sweet tooth.**
There are fossils, found in Canada,
of a **3.5-million-year-old**
bear with **tooth decay!**

10 THINGS BEARS EAT:

Acorns

Bees and beehives

Berries and other fruit

Birds and their eggs

Deer (and over 100 other kinds of mammals!)

Fish

Grass and shoots

Human trash

Pine cones

Roots ...

... and lots, lots more.

One thing they DON'T EAT is CONIFER LEAVES, such as pine needles. These are tough, waxy, and hard to digest.

～

Bears prefer young plants, which are sweeter and less tough than older ones.

Although they eat almost anything, **brown bears** are known for their AMAZING FISHING ABILITY.

They can eat **30 fat, tasty salmon** a day for a few weeks in the summer.

The bears use their **sharp claws** and strong jaws to **catch** the **fish**.

Sometimes they only **eat** the **heads** and throw the rest away.

Salmon brains are very **rich** in **fats**.

Bears usually keep themselves to
themselves, but several will gather at a
good fishing place. Sometimes the males
will **FIGHT** over the **BEST SPOT**.

**Mother bears keep their cubs
safe by staying out of the way,**
but this means they need to fish in
spots that aren't quite as good.

A mother bear will fiercely defend her cubs
from attack, even from a male bear that is much
bigger and heavier than she is.

POLAR BEARS HUNT SEALS.

Seals have
BREATHING HOLES
in the polar ice, and the bears find these ice
holes using their amazing sense of smell.

~

They wait for the seal to come up to **breathe**,
then **grab** the **seal** and **pull** it out to **eat it**.

A polar bear's **stomach** can hold a whopping **150 pounds** of meat.

That's pretty much exactly one whole seal!

AS WELL AS LARGE TEETH AND A LONG TONGUE, THE SUN BEAR HAS VERY **LONG CLAWS** FOR **TEARING** APART **TERMITE MOUNDS** BEFORE GETTING AT THE INSECTS INSIDE.

**THE SUN BEAR IS THE
ONLY BEAR THAT IS NOT
A TOP PREDATOR.**

Sun bears sometimes get eaten by
tigers, leopards, and even pythons.

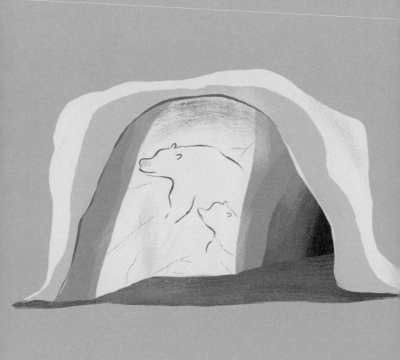

Bear Dens
and
Bear Cubs

BEARS MAKE
DENS TO SPEND
THE WINTER IN,
OR AS A NEST
WHERE THEY HAVE
THEIR CUBS.

Grizzly bears make
WINTER DENS.

The bear finds a slope, where it **digs out** a **hole** and lines it with **branches** and **leaves**. It stays there and **sleeps** for most of the **winter months**. This is called **hibernation**.

Before it gets cozy in its den, the bear has to put on a LOT of weight. It builds up its body fat by gorging on as much food as it can find.

The bear's **hibernation** is **not** such a **deep sleep** as other hibernating animals. Some scientists don't count it as hibernation at all. It **sleeps quite lightly** and can **quickly wake** up if **disturbed**.

WHEN HIBERNATING, A GRIZZLY BEAR:

∽

★ may eat nothing at all

★ gets energy from the fat it has built up

★ gets colder by around 9°F

★ has a slower heartbeat— just 8 beats per minute

★ does not poop!

THREE BEARS
THAT HIBERNATE:

American black bear

Asian black bear

Brown bear

FIVE BEARS THAT DON'T:

Panda bear

Polar bear
(except for mothers
expecting cubs)

Sloth bear

Spectacled bear

Sun bear

Sometimes.
Asian black bears
nest in trees.

POLAR BEAR MOTHERS BUILD THEIR DENS IN TIME TO SETTLE IN BEFORE WINTER ARRIVES. THE DENS ARE ONLY JUST BIGGER THAN THE BEAR, WITH A HOLE IN THE CEILING TO ALLOW FRESH AIR IN.

A DEN STAYS WARM
BECAUSE OF THE BEAR'S
BODY HEAT AND BECAUSE
THE THICK SNOW PROVIDES
AN INSULATING BLANKET.

THIS IS WHERE THE POLAR
BEAR CUBS ARE BORN AND
LOOKED AFTER. USUALLY
A MOTHER HAS TWO CUBS,
BUT SOMETIMES IT'S
ONE OR THREE.

Polar bear cubs stay in the nest for a few months, feeding on their mother's milk.

IN SPRING, THE CUBS LEAVE THE DEN, BUT AT FIRST THEY STAY CLOSE BY AND SLEEP IN THE DEN.

The cubs set off with their mother and start the long process of learning to hunt. They can catch seals at around one year old and stay with their mother until they are about two-and-a-half.

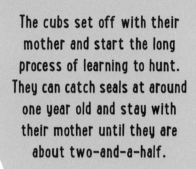

Sometimes, for example in deep snow or water, their mother carries her cubs on her back.

POLAR BEAR CUBS are
the BIGGEST BABY BEARS.
Each one weighs around
24 oz when it is born.

PANDA BABIES ARE TINY!

They are **900 times smaller** than their **mothers** and weigh just **3.5 oz at birth.** That's only about as big as two large hen's eggs.

BABY
BEARS
GROW
QUICKLY.

When it is just
three months old,
an American black
bear cub is three
times the size it
was at birth.

81

Mother bears teach their cubs to feed and climb. They will fight to protect them from danger.

Baby bears have **FUN PLAYING** with their MOTHERS and SIBLINGS.

Scientists have found that the cubs that play the most are more likely to survive to become adults.

82

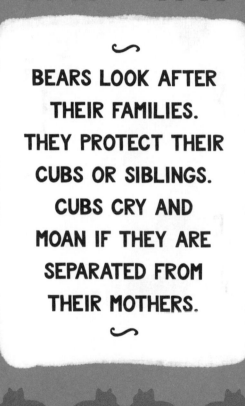

BEARS LOOK AFTER
THEIR FAMILIES.
THEY PROTECT THEIR
CUBS OR SIBLINGS.
CUBS CRY AND
MOAN IF THEY ARE
SEPARATED FROM
THEIR MOTHERS.

Amazing
Skills

Bears can **see** in **color**, which is why they can **spot** ripe fruit.

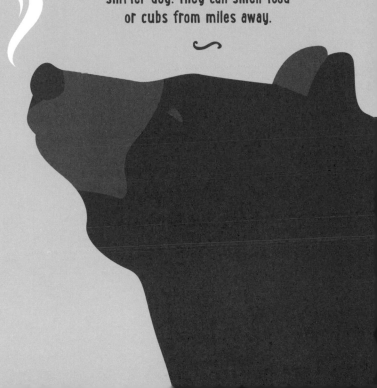

Bears have an EXCELLENT sense of smell—

seven times better even than a sniffer dog. They can smell food or cubs from miles away.

POLAR BEARS ARE CHAMPION SWIMMERS. THEY CAN...

- swim more than 60 miles without stopping
- reach speeds of 6 mph
- swim underwater and dive for over 3 minutes
- leap more than 6 ft out of the water to catch a seal.

The polar bear's scientific name is ***Ursus maritimus***, which means sea-bear.

Bears have excellent memories.

Brown bears can
remember good places to
find food after ten years!

They remember each other, too.

BEARS ARE VERY **GOOD** AT **FINDING THEIR WAY.**

Scientists think they must have a sort of **built-in compass** as well as being good at remembering landmarks.

POLAR BEARS
WASH THEMSELVES
WITH WATER OR
SNOW AFTER
THEY'VE KILLED
AND EATEN
A SEAL.

SOME BEARS USE TOOLS.
Grizzly bears pick up rocks to scratch their itchy faces.

93

A **grizzly bear** can **run as fast as** a greyhound (and faster than any human) —about **35 mph!**

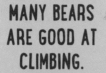

MANY BEARS ARE GOOD AT CLIMBING.

Black bears race up trees super-fast.

Heavy brown bears climb using tree branches like a ladder.

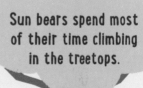

Sun bears spend most of their time climbing in the treetops.

95

Brown bears know how to cover up their SMELL.

THEY COVER THEIR TRACKS.
and sometimes they even ROLL AROUND in
STINKY ROTTEN FLESH to HIDE their own
SCENT so they can SNEAK UP on PREY.

Sometimes bears
want to send messages
with their scent.

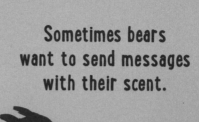

Brown bears
do a **sort of dance**
to **leave smelly
pawprints**
for other bears.

Pandas do
HANDSTANDS to
SPRAY PEE as high
as they can!

SOUNDS
BEARS USE TO
COMMUNICATE:

CLICKING AND GRUNTING— friendly

HUFFING— anxious or bothered

GROWLING AND ROARING— aggressive

BARKING— excited or alarmed

MOANING— happy or upset

Baby bears bawl, bleat, and squeal when upset, and hum when they feel safe and comfortable.

BEAR BODY LANGUAGE:

🐻 Standing on their hind legs to show how big they are and frighten others

🐻 Baring their teeth to show they're the boss

🐻 Staring to show aggression

🐻 Bowing the head or sitting down to show they're NOT being aggressive

🐻 Jumping up and down with happiness when they smell their favorite foods.

When baby sun bears play, they copy each other's facial expressions.

101

Bears and Us

Many ancient peoples worshipped bear gods and goddesses.

～

The Celts had a goddess named Artio, who was like a mother bear. The Inuits have a polar bear god named Nanook. For Finns the bear was so special it could not be mentioned by name.

～

THERE ARE BEARS IN THE STARS.

Greek myth tells of how the hunter Callisto was turned into a bear, chased and killed, and then swept away into the sky by the god Zeus. This is the constellation **Ursa Major**, or **Great Bear**. There is also **Ursa Minor**, or the **Little Bear**.

(These constellations also have other names including the Big Dipper and Little Dipper.)

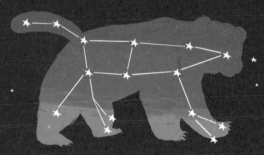

The bears in these constellations have long tails, unlike real bears.

IN WESTERN CANADA, SOMETIMES AN ALL-WHITE OR ALL-CREAM BEAR APPEARS.

It is an unusual version of a Kodiak bear, which is a variety of brown bear. Local people call these pale bears "spirit bears."

A Kitasoo/Xaisais Nation Native American story tells how Raven, the creator of everything, made a spirit bear to remind him of snow and ice when the Ice Age ended.

CHAUVET CAVE
IN SOUTHEASTERN FRANCE
CONTAINS PAINTINGS OF
ANIMALS WHICH
ARE AROUND 30,000
YEARS OLD.

The animals include reindeer,
horses, lions, hyenas ...
and bears—probably the cave
bear, which is now extinct.

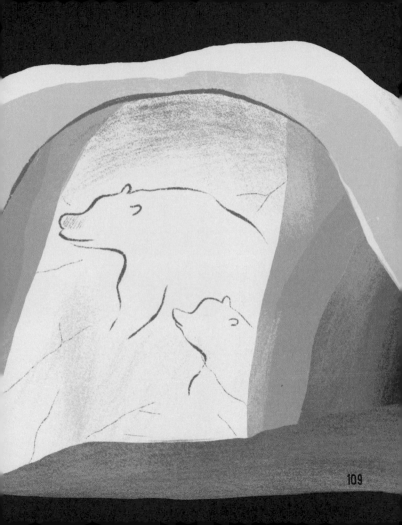

VIKING WARRIORS,
CALLED BERSERKERS,
WORE BEAR SKIN AS
PART OF THEIR BATTLE
CLOTHING, HOPING TO
MAKE THEMSELVES AS
STRONG AND FIERCE
AS A BEAR.

The expression "going beserk," meaning to get very angry and violent, comes from the berserkers.

111

The Inuit people, who live in Alaska, Greenland, and northern Canada, have hunted polar bears for thousands of years.

～

The Inuit people believe that if they treat the bears with respect, these powerful animals will allow themselves to be hunted.

～

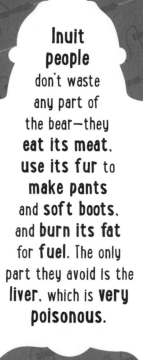

Inuit people don't waste any part of the bear—they **eat its meat**, **use its fur** to **make pants** and **soft boots**, and **burn its fat** for **fuel**. The only part they avoid is the **liver**, which is **very poisonous**.

~

EIGHT PLACES
THAT HAVE A **BEAR**
ON THEIR **FLAG,**
COAT-OF-ARMS,
OR AS THEIR
NATIONAL ANIMAL:

1. Berlin, Germany
2. Bern, Switzerland
3. California, USA
4. Finland
5. Greenland
6. Madrid, Spain
7. Montana, USA
8. Russia

THE **BEAR** CAN BE A
SYMBOL OF **STRENGTH, BRAVERY,**
AND **HEALING.**

Teddy bears are named after the US president **Theodore "Teddy" Roosevelt.** In 1902, he was out hunting when his friends **caught a black bear** cub and tied it up for him to shoot.

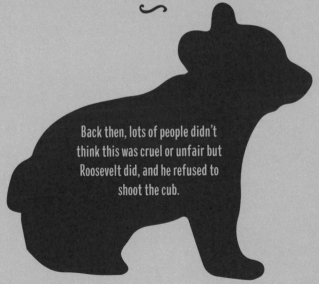

Back then, lots of people didn't think this was cruel or unfair but Roosevelt did, and he refused to shoot the cub.

A shopkeeper in New York displayed a stuffed toy bear with the label "Teddy's bear" and the name "teddy bear" grew from there.

TEN MUCH-LOVED FICTIONAL BEARS:

~

1. Baloo in The Jungle Book
2. The Care Bears
3. Fozzie Bear in The Muppets
4. Goldilocks' Three Bears
5. Iorek Byrnison, the bear king in Northern Lights
6. Lots-o'-Huggin' Bear in Toy Story 3
7. Paddington Bear
8. Po in Kung Fu Panda
9. Winnie-the-Pooh
10. Yogi Bear and Boo Boo

119

~

**THE ENGLISH
POET BYRON HAD
A PET BEAR.
WHEN HE WAS AT
UNIVERSITY, RULES
SAID HE COULD NOT
HAVE A PET DOG,
SO HE BOUGHT A
BEAR INSTEAD!**

~

AN ORPHAN BEAR NAMED WOJTEK WAS RESCUED BY POLISH SOLDIERS IN WORLD WAR II.

～

They weren't allowed pets, so they officially made him a soldier. Wojtek helped carry equipment and rose to the army rank of Corporal!

BEARS ARE IN TROUBLE BECAUSE OF HUMAN ACTIONS.

Their habitats (the places where they live) are being destroyed and they have less space to roam.

❧

The changing climate has an effect on bears' habitats, too.

The **giant panda** is the most **endangered bear.** Pandas' main food is **bamboo,** and **bamboo forests are being cut down.**

There are only around 1,600 giant pandas alive in the wild today.

Bears are hunted for all sorts of cruel purposes. They are **shot** for "sport," **caught** and **sold** as **circus acts** or **exotic pets**, and **hunted** for their beautiful fur.

IF BEARS AND HUMANS
LIVE CLOSE TOGETHER,
BEARS MIGHT BE KILLED IN
ROAD ACCIDENTS, OR SHOT
BECAUSE THEY MIGHT
ATTACK FARM ANIMALS
OR PEOPLE.

Rescue charities look after bear cubs
whose mothers have been killed. They teach
the cubs how to survive so that they can
be released back into the wild one day.

In East Asia, Asian black bears and sun bears are often **KEPT** in **FARMS** or **CAGES** in **VERY CRUEL CONDITIONS.**

One bear charity with sanctuaries in China and Vietnam has rescued 610 bears that were being treated cruelly.

The bears now have a large area to safely roam and play. With the help of caretakers and vets many of them make a full recovery from their injuries.

In January 2022, politicians in South Korea agreed to ban bear farming and said it would set up a new bear shelter and a wildlife sanctuary to protect bears.

THE ATLAS BEAR

lived in northern Africa and was hunted so widely in the 19th century that it became extinct (died out altogether).

IN ANCIENT ROME, ATLAS BEARS WERE CAUGHT IN VAST NUMBERS TO USE FOR "SPORT." SOMETIMES CRIMINALS WERE CONDEMNED TO "DEATH BY BEAR" AND WERE FORCED TO FIGHT IN FRONT OF HUGE CROWDS AGAINST BEARS, LIONS, AND TIGERS.

∽ FOUR ∽
EXTINCT BEARS:

1. ATLAS BEAR—lived in the Atlas Mountains and nearby areas of northern Africa.

2. CAVE BEAR—lived in caves throughout Europe until 24,000 years ago.

3. FLORIDA SPECTACLED BEAR—lived in North America until the end of the last ice age 10,000 years ago, and its closest living relative is today's spectacled bear.

4. SHORT-FACED BEAR—lived in North America. It had long legs, and was a bit like a grizzly bear on stilts.

Climate change is a huge problem for polar bears.

Global warming is causing **sea ice to melt**. Because they hunt on ice, this means they have to **swim even longer distances to find food**, and they are getting **exhausted**, **starving**, and even **drowning**.

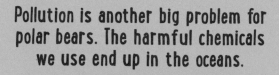

Pollution is another big problem for polar bears. The harmful chemicals we use end up in the oceans.

Fish eat them, and in turn the fish are eaten by seals and then by bears. The bears eat enough of these harmful chemicals to cause serious illness.

There is some good news. In some parts of Canada, where local people and scientists are trying to help save polar bears, the polar bears are fatter than they were 30 years ago.

EVERY YEAR, HUNDREDS OF THOUSANDS OF PEOPLE GO WALKING AND CAMPING IN AREAS WHERE THEY **MIGHT MEET BEARS.**

FIVE SIGNS A **BEAR** IS NEARBY:

1. Strands of fur on tree bark

2. Bear droppings

3. Claw marks or bite marks on tracks and trees

4. Bear footprints

5. Turned-over rocks

Bears are experts at getting at human food, even though this is bad for them. Sometimes they break into cars.

One black bear in Alaska even broke into and trashed an empty pizza delivery van parked overnight!

In 2015, a town in eastern Russia was held under siege by bears. It had been a bad year for nuts and berries and the bears in the area were desperate to find enough food for them to hibernate.

TWO BIG BEARS

MOVED INTO THE TOWN, ROAMING
THE STREETS LOOKING FOR FOOD,
RAIDING BEEHIVES, ATTACKING DOGS,
AND MAKING TOWNSPEOPLE
AFRAID TO GO OUT.

Black bears can cause problems on timber plantations because they like to **strip young trees** and eat the soft insides.

In Washington State, timber companies tackle this problem by providing food for the bears at certain times of year.

FEEDING THE BEARS MEANS FEWER TREES ARE HARMED—AND SAVES THE BEARS FROM BEING SHOT.

But the bears get used to being around humans, which means they are more likely to eat food packaging, and more in danger of being hit by cars.

137

BEARS DO NOT GET
ON VERY WELL IN
ZOOS. THEY ARE VERY
INTELLIGENT AND NEED
HUGE AREAS TO LIVE
IN SO THAT THEY CAN
LIVE WELL AND BE
HEALTHY.

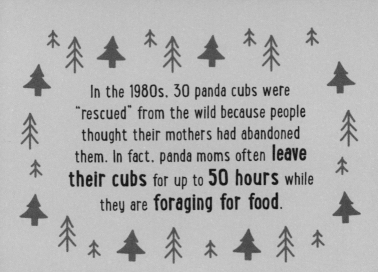

In the 1980s, 30 panda cubs were "rescued" from the wild because people thought their mothers had abandoned them. In fact, panda moms often **leave their cubs** for up to **50 hours** while they are **foraging for food**.

PEOPLE OFTEN THINK THAT PANDAS ARE NOT VERY GOOD AT HAVING CUBS AT ALL, but they do fine in the wild. Like most bears, they find it difficult to have cubs in captivity.

Panda experts think it is important to keep some pandas in zoos.

If we help them to have babies who will grow healthy and strong, we may be able to release them into the wild one day and boost their numbers overall.

In 2020, there were around **600 giant pandas living in zoos** around the world and 44 panda babies were born that year.

Protecting the giant panda's habitat is an even better way to try to save this beautiful animal.

THE **GOBI BEAR** IS A VERY RARE VARIETY OF BROWN BEAR.

It lives in the mountain desert areas of Mongolia in Asia. In 2014, there were just 29 of them left in the world.

THE GOOD NEWS
~ IS THAT ~

a Gobi Bear Project was set up to
help save them. Their habitat is now a
protected area and scientists are finding
out what illnesses and problems they
might have, and how to help them.
In 2020, there were **40 bears.**